W9-AWF-054

HOW & WHY ?

SEEDS TRAVEL

Elaine Pascoe is the author of more than 20 acclaimed children's books on a wide range of subjects.
Dwight Kuhn's scientific expertise and artful eye work together with the camera to capture the awesome wonder of the natural world.

Please visit our web site at: www.garethstevens.com
For a free color catalog describing Gareth Stevens Publishing's list of high-quality books
and multimedia programs, call 1-800-542-2595 or fax your request to (414) 332-3567.

Library of Congress Cataloging-in-Publication Data

Pascoe, Elaine.
    Seeds travel / by Elaine Pascoe; photographs by Dwight Kuhn. — North American ed.
      p. cm. — (How & why: a springboards into science series)
    Includes bibliographical references and index.
    Summary: Briefly describes some of the different ways various kinds of seeds are carried
from place to place to find good places to grow.
    ISBN 0-8368-3012-1 (lib. bdg.)
    1. Seeds—Dispersal—Juvenile literature. [1. Seeds—Dispersal.] I. Kuhn, Dwight, ill. II. Title.
QK929.P37   2002
581.4'67—dc21   2001049486

This North American edition first published in 2002 by
Gareth Stevens Publishing
A World Almanac Education Group Company
330 West Olive Street, Suite 100
Milwaukee, WI 53212 USA

First published in the United States in 2000 by Creative Teaching Press, Inc., P.O. Box 2723, Huntington Beach, CA 92647-0723.
Text © 2000 by Elaine Pascoe. All photographs © 2000 by Dwight Kuhn, except dog photo on p. 11 © 2000 by David Kuhn/Dwight
Kuhn. Additional end matter © 2002 by Gareth Stevens, Inc.

Gareth Stevens editor: Mary Dykstra
Gareth Stevens designer: Tammy Gruenewald

Printed in the United States of America

1 2 3 4 5 6 7 8 9 06 05 04 03 02

HOW & WHY❓

SEEDS TRAVEL

by Elaine Pascoe
photographs by Dwight Kuhn

A SPRINGBOARDS INTO
SCIENCE
SERIES

Gareth Stevens Publishing
A WORLD ALMANAC EDUCATION GROUP COMPANY

An apple falls to the ground. As weeks go by, the apple rots, and seeds that were inside the apple's core are lying on the ground.

The seeds sprout, and new apple trees begin to grow. But a seed can sprout and grow only if it is in the right place — a place with enough soil, sunlight, and water.

Sometimes a seed must travel to find the right place to grow. Often, animals help. When a chipmunk finds a strawberry, it feasts on the tasty fruit. A chipmunk eats the whole strawberry — seeds and all. Later, the strawberry seeds will be dropped on the ground in the chipmunk's waste.

Squirrels help seeds travel, too. In fall,
squirrels gather acorns, which are the
seeds of oak trees. Squirrels bury
the acorns so they will
have food in winter.

But squirrels do not always come back to eat their buried stores of food. Some of the acorns squirrels leave in the ground sprout in spring.

Some seeds are hitchhikers. Burdock seeds grow in clusters that look like spiny balls. Each seed has a spine, and each spine has a tiny hook at the end.

The hooks catch on anything that touches them — a dog's fur, your clothes, or even a duckling's soft feathers. Then the seeds are carried away, hitching a ride to a new place where they might grow.

The wind helps many seeds travel. The seeds of maple trees have winged cases called samaras covering them.

When samaras catch a breeze, they carry their seeds away from the maple tree where the seeds formed. Seeds that land in the right places will sprout, and new maple trees will begin to grow.

Dandelion seeds float along on fluffy little parachutes. These seeds are very small and light, so they float easily in the air.

When the wind blows, dandelion seeds rise up into the air like a cloud. The seeds may travel very far before they finally land and sprout.

This pretty wildflower is a jewelweed plant. Jewelweed is also called "touch-me-not." Can you guess why?

If you touch a jewelweed's ripe seedpod, the pod springs open, and the seeds inside shoot out like little rockets! If the seeds land in the right places, new jewelweed plants will grow.

Can you answer these "HOW & WHY" questions?

1. Why does a seed travel?

2. How do squirrels store food for winter?

3. How do burdock seeds hitch a ride?

4. How do the wings of maple seeds help them travel?

5. Why do dandelion seeds float so easily?

6. Why is a jewelweed plant called "touch-me-not"?

(See page 20 for answers.)

ANSWERS

1. A seed travels to find a good place to grow, which is a place that has enough soil, sunlight, and water.

2. In fall, squirrels gather acorns from oak trees and bury them in the ground.

3. When the tiny hooks on the tips of burdock seeds catch on people's clothing or animals' fur, these hitchhiking seeds get a free ride.

4. When the wings of maple seeds catch a breeze, the seeds fly through the air, carried by wind.

5. Dandelion seeds are very small and light, and they have fluffy little parachutes to help them float in the air.

6. If you touch the ripe seedpod of a jewelweed plant, the pod splits open, and the seeds shoot out.

Sock It to 'Em

To study seeds, all you need is an old sock that is large enough to fit over your shoe! With an adult, visit an area that has a lot of dry grass and weeds. Pull the sock over one of your shoes and walk through the weeds. Then take off the sock and keep it in a plastic bag until you get home. At home, gently shake the sock and the bag over a piece of paper. How many different kinds of seeds did the sock collect? Did any seeds stick to the sock after you shook it? Examine the seeds and sort them into groups. Find out how these kinds of seeds normally travel.

Sail Away

The samaras that hold maple seeds have a special shape that helps them travel through the air. To see how they work, cut a strip of paper about 8 inches (20 centimeters) long and 1 inch (2.5 cm) wide. Fold the strip in half, then fold one end over so it points to the right. Turn the whole strip over and fold the other end to the right to make a "T" shape. Attach a paper clip to the fold at the bottom of the "T". Throw your paper samara into the air and watch what happens.

Blowing in the Wind

Like dandelions, milkweed plants have seeds with built-in parachutes so they can travel by air. Unlike dandelions, milkweed seeds develop inside pods. In fall, look for milkweed pods on a walk in the country or at a nature center. If possible, open a pod for a closer look at the seeds and their parachutes. After you examine the seeds, blow them into the air and watch them travel.

GLOSSARY

breeze: a light wind.

burdock: a type of weed with spiny seeds that grow in ball-like clusters, called burrs, and spread by sticking to fur or clothing.

bury: to put something into the ground and cover it with dirt.

cases: containers to hold and protect things.

clusters (n): tightly gathered groups.

duckling: a baby duck or a young duck.

feasts (v): eats a large amount of rich and tasty food.

float (v): to move along by resting on the surface of a liquid or by drifting in the air.

fluffy: light and soft like a cotton ball or the feathers of a baby bird.

gather: collect, a little at a time, and bring together in one place.

hitchhikers: people or things that travel by getting a free ride from someone or by being carried by some other moving force.

rots: spoils and decays, or falls apart.

samaras: the hard, dry fruits of some kinds of trees, such as maples, that carry seeds inside and have wings attached.

seedpod: a shell or casing that grows on a plant and holds the plant's seeds inside it.

spiny: having stiff, sharp, hairlike growths that stick out like thorns.

sprout (v): to begin growing.

stores (n): supplies kept on hand to be used when they are needed.

waste (n): the unused substances left over after food has been digested, and which leaves the body as a liquid or a solid.

More Books to Read

Berries, Nuts, and Seeds. Young Naturalist Field Guides (series). Diane L. Burns (Gareth Stevens)
Dandelion Adventures. L. Patricia Kite (Millbrook Press)
Maple Tree. Sunflower. Life Cycles (series). David M. Schwartz (Gareth Stevens)
Plant Fruits & Seeds. Look Once, Look Again (series). David M. Schwartz (Gareth Stevens)
The Science of Plants. Jonathan Bocknek (Gareth Stevens)
Seeds. Gail Saunders-Smith (Pebble Books)

Videos

How Seeds Get Here ... and There. (MBG Videos)
The Magic School Bus Goes to Seed: Growing Places with Plants. (Scholastic)
The Private Life of Plants: Branching Out. (Turner)

Web Sites

tqjunior.thinkquest.org/3715/seeds4.html
waynesword.palomar.edu/plfeb99.htm
www.geocities.com/CapeCanaveral/Hall/1244/llavorangles1.htm

Some web sites stay current longer than others. For additional web sites, use a good search engine to locate the following topics: *seed dispersal, seeds,* and *spreading seeds.*

INDEX